100+
REASONS TO
READ BOOKS

CHARLES MWEWA

ACP
PRESS

Ottawa, 2021

DEDICATION

For

Emmerance.

CONTENTS

AUTHOR'S WORDS

Knowledge is never centralized. It comes in snippets and clips from different people. Progress means three things: Learn, believe and act. All of these are triggered by reading, different topics and interests. You can't succeed beyond the knowledge you currently have. You can't be better than what you don't know. Those who read widely, will eventually be better prepared, better informed and will be more decisive. Invest in books and actually read. The wisdom of God and of humans is transmitted in these pages. Don't depend on anyone to read for you - it's they who will grow and make progress, and NOT you. Good readers make better leaders. Read, read, and read - all the time.

This little book is for everyone, especially for those who desire to reach further than time and tour the minds, through books.

100+ REASONS

1.   Knowledge is never centralized. It comes in snippets and clips from different people.

2.   Progress means three things: Learn, believe and act. All of these are triggered by reading, different topics and interests.

3. You can't succeed beyond the knowledge you currently have.

4.   You can't be better than what you don't know.

5.   Those who read widely, will eventually be better prepared, better informed and will be more decisive.

6.   Invest in books and read. The wisdom of God and of humans is transmitted in these pages.

7.   Don't depend on anyone to read for you - it's them or they who will grow and make progress, and NOT you.

8.   Good readers make better leaders.

9.   Read, read, and read - all the time, and be well-served.

10. Reading travels faster than jets – you can reach places money can't afford.

11. Reading is
the tourism of
the mind.

12.   The more
     you know, the
     longer you will
     live, relatively
     speaking.

13. It is what you don't know that kills you, faster.

14.   Books are
      libraries of
      memories and
      wise nuggets.

15.   The mind is like an elastic band – with reading, it stretches longer and further.

16.   Reading fights and conquers distress – pain, anguish and stress.

17. Books contain the collective wisdom of many experiences.

18. The more you read, the readier you become.

19. It is good
reading that
assists in
memory
retention.

20. Readers
eventually
become
competent
analysts.

21. Reading books boosts analytical skills.

22. Reading improves thinking; good readers become ardent thinkers.

23. The reader is a passionate experimenter – experimentation discovers the world.

24. Reading
    books enhances
    motor cognitive
    skills.

25. Reading, literacy, is a weapon against poverty.

26.   There is no sustainable freedom without knowledge, without reading.

27. The reading process engages the brain in ways that make the brain happy.

28. A happy brain is a bank of ideas – most of progressive ideas come from reading.

29. Keep reading and keep becoming.

30.   The more
      you read, the
      better your
      critical faculties
      get.

31. Only great and enthusiastic readers provoke changes that reshape society.

32. Reading will free you from the shackles of mental and psychological slavery.

33. You may not be abused arbitrarily if you are well-informed.

34. Dictators reign longer in illiterate societies; readers will rebel.

35. Read your way to higher promotion.

36. Reading increases your verbal efficacy — you eventually become a better communicator.

37.   The reader will have their ears sharper, more attentive and more receptive.

38. Reading improves concentration – no doubt about that.

39. The key difference between the "developed" and the "developing" formations, is that the former read, and the later are still trying to.

40. Reading improves self-expression.

41. Reading is a self-motivation pill.

42. Most gems
 are hidden in the
 pages of great
 books, discover
 yours by reading.

43. Walk where the greatest minds have walked, read their books.

44.   Every book
   was written with
   you in mind.

45.   Books are like a gold mine; you only benefit from it by digging it out.

46. Buy, borrow, and by all means get a book and read it, in it may be preserved your very survival.

47.   Only reading books makes you think older than your age.

48. Reading finetunes your response sensibilities.

49. Hopeless are those who don't know how to read; regrettable are those who have no books to read; but woe to those who know how to

read, have the
chances to read
and don't take
any.

50.   Any book, no matter how poor it might have been written, may have at least one fact or nugget or truth that is helpful to the reader; the

secret is in
reading and
discovering it.

51. Stories make the world go round; everything that is entertaining, educative, or even disparaging, may probably be written in a book somewhere.

52. When great minds want to leave a legacy behind, they usually leave it in a book.

53. Books changed the world when the printing press was discovered; and now, they change the world further with the discovery of an eBook format.

54.   A right book
   at the right time,
   may just be the
   thing you need
   to save your life.

55. Authors are
   like seed-sowers;
   they spread
   knowledge
   nuggets into
   people's souls –
   some yield a ten,
   others a hundred
   fold.

56. Books open up doors that a good education or a rich background might not.

57. Reading books helps nonentities share in the glory of winning.

58. There is no lock known to humanity that reading many books cannot open.

59. Readers are rarely lost; they always find their way.

60. Perspective is uneven unless you learn to understand others through books.

61. Reading
     books widens
     one's perspective
     and makes them
     a better person.

62.   People who read widely and frequently, also understand others better.

 100+ Reasons

63. Reading helps
one understand
the struggles of
others and the
joys that go
around in a
closed world.

64.   Reading increases one's vocabulary so that they can relate to any speech interest.

65. The best way to become a universal citizen is to read books about many subjects.

66. If you want to conquer anything, read a book or books about it.

67. Books and money have one thing in common; they are both valueless unless they are used.

68. Jesus said, "For truly I tell you, until heaven and earth disappear, not the smallest letter, not the least stroke of a pen, will by any

means disappear
from the law
until everything
is
accomplished."
He was right,
books will
survive the
apocalypse.

69. While on earth, Jesus used a book to defeat the devil, when he answered, "It is written!"

70. The easiest way to understand others, and, therefore, to be empathetic and sympathetic, is through reading many books on

many topics and
interests,
thereby, being
able to interact
with diverse
emotions,
feelings, interests
and
backgrounds.

71. homophobes, racists and xenophobes are usually people who rarely read about their victims.

72. The more
     you read about
     something, the
     more lovely it
     begins to be.

73.   People who read books are rarely "Yes, yes men."

74. When you give someone money, they can only buy one or two ideas; but when you give someone a good book, they can birth many ideas.

75. Readers are also usually very smart people.

76. Reading and intelligence are co-relatives.

77. Teachers know this: The most intelligent students in their classrooms was also an avid reader.

78.   The only way you can be better than your teacher is when you read more books than they did.

79. Books are always speaking. Are you always listening? They are always teaching. Are you always learning?

100+ Reasons

80. If you want to experience it, read about it.

81. Books improve your level of expectation and elevate you towards divine manumission; faith comes by reading.

82. Artistic
genius is a
symbol of
textual mastery;
good readers
also become
better actors.

83. Reading helps you to discover many ways of doing things.

84. Things are only complex before you read about them.

85. Haven't you noticed that most people fall asleep as they read a good book? Yes, because reading is a sleep-aid.

86. Reading is one of the commonest definitions of enjoyment.

87. When reading reaches its term, it gives birth to happiness.

88. Most readers are happy people.

89. Reading good books takes bad thoughts away and helps to relax tense muscles.

90. Wisdom comes from reading; the more books you read, the wiser you get.

91. Except in some sports, good readers may also earn a relatively higher income.

92. Reading is sexy; those who read more, may also be more attractive.

93. Reading books inspires one to be and do things they would never imagine they could do.

94. Reading is
the manure of
the brain.

95. Reading books, especially novels, expands one's vision.

96. Reading books is part of a lifetime of continuous learning.

97. Reading builds other skills, such as attentive listening, interpersonal relationships, improved communication,

social
competence, and
stimuli-response
assertiveness.

98. Reading improves judgment making abilities.

99. Reading good
books makes
one prescient;
because
discernment
thrives in the
reading
atmosphere.

100. Reading makes you a better writer.

101. Read
    especially books
    in the following
    genres: novels
    (helps you to live
    longer); science
    (exposes you to
    practical reality);
    philosophy
    (helps you to

breed useful ideas); religion (gives you peace of mind and prepares you for the after-life); arts (makes you creative); financial (helps you to conquer poverty and become financially independent);

politics (helps you to remain relevant to your locale, region or nation); personal interest and motivational (helps you to utilize your God-given abilities and talents); news and current affairs (helps you to manage your present well); and comics (helps you to smile, laugh, dance and generally, invigorates happiness). Be versatile, multifaceted, sophisticated, inquisitive and curious. Read and lead.

102. We all don't live forever, we die. There are three things you can leave behind as a legacy or inheritance for your children: Properties

(especially real estate, such as houses); securities (bonds, stocks, debentures, secure investments, or money); or BOOKS. Majority of the people don't have properties to leave behind,

and many people
don't own
securities.
However,
everyone can
buy, keep and
spare a book for
their children.
When their
children read the
books they left
behind, those
children would
inherit valuable

knowledge to make them live, at least, better than their parents lived. Begin buying, reading and creating your personal library today.

14-DAY READING PLAN

DAY 1

Read this same book:

- Write down what you learned:

_____

_____

_____

_____

_____

_____

_____

_____

_____

_____

_____

_____

_____

100+ Reasons **DAY 2**

Take time to find a library/ies:

- List down all the libraries
  you found:

  _____
  _____
  _____
  _____
  _____
  _____
  _____
  _____
  _____
  _____
  _____
  _____
  _____
  _____

Find and read a good novel:

- Write down your personal
  review of the novel:

  _____
  _____
  _____
  _____
  _____
  _____
  _____
  _____
  _____
  _____
  _____
  _____
  _____

Find and read a good science book:

- How does this book enhance the knowledge of your material surroundings?

  _____
  _____
  _____
  _____
  _____
  _____
  _____
  _____
  _____
  _____
  _____
  _____
  _____

DAY 5

Find and read a good philosophy book:

- Did you learn something about wisdom – write down your view:

_____

_____

_____

_____

_____

_____

_____

_____

_____

_____

_____

_____

100+ Reasons DAY 6

Find and read a good religious book:

- Did you learn something about God – write down your personal faith statement:

_____

_____

_____

_____

_____

_____

_____

_____

_____

_____

_____

_____

100+ Reasons **DAY 7**

Find and read a good book on law:

- Did you learn something about your rights and responsibilities – write down where you may go to seek for legal help when in need:

_____

_____

_____

_____

_____

_____

_____

_____

_____

_____

_____

Find and read a good mathematics or networking or programming book:

- Did you learn something about structures and networks – write down your knowledge of how the Internet connects us and impacts our information sharing and privacy:

  _____

  _____

  _____

  _____

  _____

  _____

  _____

  _____

  _____

DAY 9

Find and read a good personal
growth/motivational book:

- Did you discover
  something about your
  abilities, talents or dreams –
  write down your
  vision/mission or personal
  statement:

  _____
  _____
  _____
  _____
  _____
  _____
  _____
  _____
  _____
  _____
  _____
  _____

Find and read any book that
interests you:

- Did you learn something
  about anything – write
  down your experience:

  _____

  _____

  _____

  _____

  _____

  _____

  _____

  _____

  _____

  _____

  _____

  _____

  _____

  _____

  _____

Book legacy:

- Have you ever thought about your future – write down the kinds of books you want to leave behind for your children:

_____
_____
_____
_____
_____
_____
_____
_____
_____
_____
_____
_____
_____

Investing in books:

- How much does a good book cost – plan how you can be buying at least one good book every month for your library:

  _____

  _____

  _____

  _____

  _____

  _____

  _____

  _____

  _____

  _____

  _____

  _____

  _____

  _____

Donating/giving a book:

- Do you know anyone you think might need a good book to read and grow – list important milestones like birthdays, weddings, graduations, and etc., of people in your immediate circle, and commit to giving them a book on their special day:

_____

_____

_____

_____

_____

_____

_____

_____

_____

DAY 14

Start from Day 1 all over:

- Do the same things you did from Day 1 to Day 13 (this time read books on art, comics, psychology, sociology, geography, history, culture, special education, politics, economics and finances, and etc., – did anything improve about you – list everything you improved in:

INDEX

CHARLES MWEWA

Charles Mwewa (LLM – cand.) is a Dad, a husband, a prolific author and researcher, poet, novelist, political thinker, a law professor, and Christian and community leader. Mwewa has written no less than 30 books and counting. Mwewa, his wife and their three daughters, reside in the Canadian Capital City of Ottawa.

AUTHOR'S CONTACT

Email Address:

spynovel2016@gmail.com

Facebook:

www.facebook.com/charlesmwewa

Twitter:

https://twitter.com/BooksMwewa

Instagram:

instagram.com/mwewabooks/?hl=en

Author's Website:

https://www.charlesmwewa.com

www.ingramcontent.com/pod-product-compliance
Lightning Source LLC
Chambersburg PA
CBHW071805090426
42737CB00012B/1952